AROUND
AMESBURY
IN OLD PHOTOGRAPHS

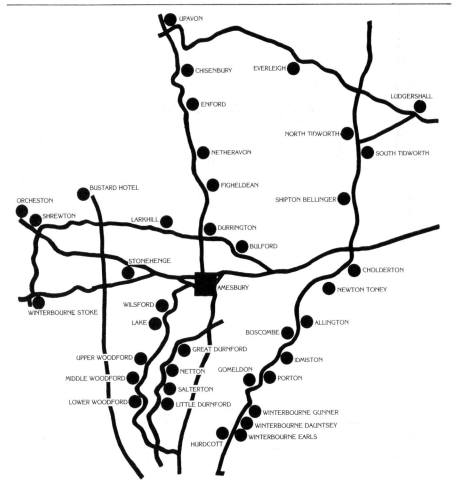

UPAVON
CHISENBURY
EVERLEIGH
LUDGERSHALL
ENFORD
NORTH TIDWORTH
NETHERAVON
SOUTH TIDWORTH
BUSTARD HOTEL
FIGHELDEAN
SHIPTON BELLINGER
ORCHESTON
SHREWTON
LARKHILL
DURRINGTON
STONEHENGE
BULFORD
CHOLDERTON
AMESBURY
NEWTON TONEY
WILSFORD
WINTERBOURNE STOKE
LAKE
ALLINGTON
BOSCOMBE
GREAT DURNFORD
UPPER WOODFORD
IDMISTON
NETTON
GOMELDON
MIDDLE WOODFORD
PORTON
SALTERTON
LOWER WOODFORD
LITTLE DURNFORD
WINTERBOURNE GUNNER
WINTERBOURNE DAUNTSEY
WINTERBOURNE EARLS
HURDCOTT

OUR MAP, drawn by Lisa Daniels, shows the locations around Amesbury which are featured in this, the fourth in our series of books depicting south-east Wiltshire in old photographs. Further volumes are planned to include the hamlets and villages to the south and west of Wilton. (Map not to scale).

AROUND AMESBURY
IN OLD PHOTOGRAPHS

COLLECTED BY
PETER DANIELS

ALAN SUTTON

Alan Sutton Publishing Limited
Phoenix Mill · Far Thrupp · Stroud · Gloucestershire

First Published 1990

British Library Cataloguing in Publication Data

Around Amesbury in old photographs.
1. Wiltshire. Amesbury, history
I. Daniels, Peter *1948–*
942.319

ISBN 0-86299-799-2

Typeset in 9/10 Korinna.
Typesetting and origination by
Alan Sutton Publishing Limited.
Printed in Great Britain by
Dotesios Printers Limited.

CONTENTS

PETER DANIELS, 'THE OLD PICTURE DETECTIVE', seen here with an 1894 Crypto safety cycle from the Charlie Knight Collection. This interesting machine was restored by Charlie in the early 1960s. (Photograph courtesy of Russell Emm.)

INTRODUCTION

This book is the third in the series to have been compiled by Peter Daniels and he presents a selection of material which is commendable for its breadth and depth. The reader is taken around the eastern half of Salisbury Plain along the courses of the rivers Avon, Bourne and Till and, during the journey, thirty-six rural communities and Stonehenge are visited.

One of the cries often heard today is that of how quickly life races by. The ease of communication, the speed and reliability of transport, the good roads, all contribute to facilitate the process of modern life but in so doing help to create the multitude of diversions which now consume our precious time. By turning the pages of this book the itinerary of its journey can be completed at a speed in keeping with the pace of life today. But in attempting the exercise a metamorphosis may take place, with the discerning reader being slowed and drawn into the very life under observation.

Within the pages practically every aspect of daily life in the villages is recorded. The day-to-day activities of a community are covered, alongside those with wider connotations. Thus we see the various trades and professions: the blacksmith, carpenter, butcher, baker, grocer, chemist and so on, plus the centre for community news – the post office. The world of commerce is also represented. The need for reliable transport was a feature of the times and we are shown a glimpse of its development; steam traction, the carrier – an essential feature of any community – buses, taxis and the railways that were instrumental in forming new horizons for travel and trade. Also, that very latest mode of transport, the aeroplane. Its early association with Salisbury Plain was unfortunately a product of war; its infancy as a science is recorded on the roadside and in fields by the several memorials to aircrews.

The principal employment was agriculture, represented here by the typical activities of dairying, planting and harvesting. Achievement was an essential feature as it established one's place in society and was of benefit to one's employer – hence we see the feat of Cherry the champion cow recorded! A day's work was long and demanding; pay was low and, earlier, diet poor. After work it was off to the inn, or pub, to talk about jobs and bosses or, with the help of the landlord, to forget the lack of them! The pubs, inns and hotels are here as well – from the humble establishment catering for the labourer, to the new venture catering for the railway traveller, and larger hotels for the more sophisticated customer.

To partially compensate for the hard times there was, of course, religion and recreation. The religious tone that we see is one of strong evangelism. There was a need to save people from the evils of the time, thus we have the Sunday schools, the Temperance groups much in evidence and, to remove every last excuse for non-attendance at a service, the motor chapel! Now that could prove an interesting revival if it were ever resurrected! The effort put into recreational pastimes must surely indicate their importance, albeit unspoken: the fairs, fêtes, carnivals and bands evolved from traditions going far back into time. But we have modern variants as well – the dance band, amateur dramatics, carnivals to raise funds for the new hospitals. Also the team activities through which a village's prestige could be expressed – football, tug-of-war and so on. Friendly Societies and working men's clubs were formed with the annual treat of a charabanc outing to some far and 'exotic' venue.

There is also, of course, the more sombre side of life depicted. One sees the growth of the military establishments around the Plain and the presence of British and foreign military personnel. The opportunities for work in building the airfields, military garrisons and countless huts must have been immense. The social, religious and recreational facilities, created to help relieve the soldier's onerous burden, were a necessary feature. Exciting times, except when the dreaded telegrams were received. The funeral of Sir Edmund Antrobus, Amesbury's manorial Lord, is recorded, an event resulting from the death of his own son in the First World War. People important to a community were remembered at their deaths, and due dignity was accorded at their funerals; thus we see the sad occasions for Mr Kirby the fireman and Mr Sheers the bandsman. Nor could a community avoid its natural disasters; thus we are shown typical scenes of fire, flood and snowfall.

All these things are going on within the pages of this book. However, the moment a page is opened activity ceases and the occupants of a scene turn to view the intruder. What the reader will see, in spite of all the hardships described, are people who are not afraid to be scrutinized and who have composed themselves with dignity for the camera. A family group or person or pet will return your inspection with a quiet gaze waiting for the page to be turned again. One thing that will not be seen is the person who made the book possible – the rural photographer; it is the professional skill of that person which allows us to enjoy this brief glimpse back into our history.

Peter Goodhugh
August 1990

SECTION ONE

Amesbury

SOUTH MILL, 1904. William Sandell had been working this watermill since the first half of the last century. At the time of our photograph, however, he had retired in favour of his son William junior who in turn was succeeded by his son Thomas.

THE FUNERAL OF COLONEL SIR EDMUND ANTROBUS BT, 15 February 1915. For some weeks Sir Edmund had been feeling unwell, he never really recovered from the shock of losing his only son pictured below.

EDMUND ANTROBUS. The only son and heir of Sir Edmund Antrobus 4th Bt. A lieutenant in the Grenadier Guards, Edmund was killed in action during the first Battle of Ypres in October 1914.

THE FUNERAL OF JOHN SHEERS, June 1933. John was an enthusiastic member of the Amesbury band, his colleagues are pictured here pulling the bier past his former home in Parsonage Lane.

JOHN SHEERS (1902–33). For many years John was employed as an agricultural worker by Messrs Wort and Way at Redhouse Farm, Amesbury. Among his comrades in the picture above are bandsmen Charles Fowler, Edgar Harrison, and Reginald Thorne.

AMESBURY PARISH COUNCILLORS, 1921–4. Back row, left to right: George Scott, Sydney Hinxman (gardener), William Hough (clockmaker), Thomas Matthews (general builder), William Witt (shopkeeper), William Mundy and Hubert William Lever Eyres (carrier). Left to right, in the front row: James Martin (nurseryman), Frederick Hale (shopkeeper and vice chairman), Harry James (chairman), Sir Cosmo Gordon Antrobus Bt and Stanley Bigwood (accountant).

THE WESTON FAMILY in 1914. John and Fanny had five children: three boys (pictured here) and two girls. Jack, the eldest son, can be seen to the left with Archie in the centre and Derrick to the right.

HUBERT FREDERICK EYRES AND ELSIE MAY ZEBEDEE on their wedding day, 27 April 1922. The gentleman pictured third from the right in the back row is Elsie's father, Albert Zebedee. Rose Zebedee is seated far right and Frances Kate Eyres, Hubert's stepmother, is to the left of the same row.

HAROLD, RALPH AND ERNIE EYRES. In September 1911 the boys were photographed in the garden of their Church Street home.

13

THE ZEBEDEE FAMILY in 1910. From left to right, in the back row: Beatrice (eldest child), Arthur, Charles (their father), May and Albert. In the front row, left to right: William ('Bill'), Emma (Charles' wife), Annie, Edith (youngest) and Elsie. The family lived in Flower Lane.

SYDNEY HINXMAN AND HIS WIFE, photographed in the garden of their Salisbury Street home sometime before the First World War. Sydney was employed as a gardener by Sir Cosmo Antrobus.

THREE GENERATIONS OF THE CROOK FAMILY, in June 1943, seen here at Viney's Farmhouse. Isaac Charles Crook is pictured with his eldest son, Norman Charles, and his grandson, Richard Charles (Norman's eldest son). The Crooks have been farming in Amesbury since 1917 and Richard carries on the family tradition.

PHILIP WESTON'S SHOP IN FLOWER LANE. Situated near the old weighbridge, Philip is pictured here with his wife 'Auntie'. The business was started before the First World War and continued until around 1936.

SALISBURY STREET in 1910. The thatched wall to the left has gone and Logan Homecare now trade here. The dwelling to the extreme right was at one time occupied by Thomas Creed, an employee of the Antrobus Estate. Herbert Fellender, chauffeur to Sir Cosmo Antrobus, lived in the building adjacent to the cart.

THE VILLAGE BAKER AND GROCERY STORES in 1927. Harry Jenkins and his wife stand in the doorway of their Salisbury Street shop. The firm's second-hand Ford Model T delivery van (HR 2203) was originally a touring car owned by William Malone of the Bell Hotel.

HERBERT MOORE'S OUTFITTER AND BOOT STORES, pictured here in Salisbury Street before the First World War. At the time a good pair of boots would cost anything between 9s. and 13s. 6d. This shop is now Zebedee's the butchers.

CHURCH STREET, during the late 1920s. The proprietors of the Avon Hotel were the Misses Fownes. Travellers and passers-by could not help but notice the signs fixed near the main entrance; 'Dinners, Teas and Luncheons served'. A Morris van from Liptons of Salisbury was delivering wholesale teas and groceries.

THE CHURCH STREET HOME OF THE AMESBURY CARRIER. When this photograph was taken in around 1900 Hubert 'Cooky' Eyres' business was well established. A sign on the wall of his house advertises his service. 'Eyres, Amesbury & Salisbury Carrier. Tuesdays, Thursdays and Saturdays'. The family later moved down the street to Weycot.

THE HIGH STREET in 1903. To the right of our picture is the Amesbury Gaol. A notice on the wall warned people to 'Stick No Bills' but someone had ignored it and fixed three posters there. The message was clear for everyone to see, 'Recruits Wanted for the Wiltshire Regiment'.

RICHARD DICKENSON & COMPANY, in the High Street. The firm, pictured here before 1907, were military purveyors who hired out marquees and other catering requisites. The locations of their ten branches were listed across the top of their Amesbury warehouse which is shown in its entirety in the picture on the top of this page.

HIGH STREET, at around the time of the First World War. The vehicle standing outside Salisbury Plain Motors is a 15 hp Scout car made in Salisbury. John Weston was responsible for the neat piles of dust along the left hand side of the road. He kept the streets spotlessly clean for many years. You can see a picture of John with his wife and three sons on page 12.

NORTON MOTOR CYCLES AT SLOAN'S GARAGE, pictured here in the High Street between the wars. The business, started by the Sloan family before 1920, was operating for almost fifty years. The two young men to the left of the photograph are not known to us, the other lads are Andrew Sloan, David Sloan, Stan Dibben and Freddy Flay.

A DAIMLER WAGONETTE AT THE GEORGE HOTEL. When this photograph was taken in 1904 Melville Whistler was proprietor of this 'Commercial & Family Hotel and Posting House'. 'Open & Closed Carriages, Brakes and Wagonettes let out on hire. Good Stabling and Loose Boxes. Headquarters of the hawking club.'

SIDNEY TAMBLING'S AMESBURY SUPPLY STORES at 25 High Street. A 'guess the weight' contest was in full swing when this photograph was taken in the twenties. Do you have any idea who won the competition by correctly estimating the weight of the two live beasts that are being displayed in the doorway?

SMITHFIELD STREET AND THE ENTRANCE TO COLDHARBOUR, in around 1906. John Barnes' hostelry, the Greyhound Inn, can be seen to the right and to the left is George Bailey's dairy-cart which carried a seventeen-gallon milk churn.

THE WAR MEMORIAL AND ENTRANCE TO AMESBURY HOUSE. The house was demolished around twenty-five years ago and the grounds are now occupied by The Centre, Library and Health Centre. William 'Bill' Worsdell's Austin taxi is parked to the left of the memorial.

IVYDEAN PRIVATE HOTEL AND AMESBURY POST OFFICE in 1904. Mrs Ann Lucretia Fleming was proprietress of the guest-house and Thomas Merchant was sub-postmaster. Letters were delivered at 11.45 a.m. and 6.55 p.m. Monday to Saturday, but from around 4.40 p.m. only on Sundays. The guest-house was destroyed by fire on 10 June 1911.

THE DAY AFTER THE FIRE. Photographers arrived from all over the district to take pictures of the ruins. Many of their photographs were printed on postcards and from the hundreds that were sold quite a number have survived. This is one of them.

CORONATION DECORATIONS IN SALISBURY STREET, 1911. The proprietors of Ye Olde Shoppe Bakery, pictured above, proudly display the words 'God Bless our Queen'. In the lower picture several gaily festooned cars can be seen outside Jerome's Coachworks and Collins' Cycle Depot. Union Jacks and red, white and blue bunting adorn most buildings.

WILTS. & DORSET MOTOR SERVICES, incorporated in January 1915. Pictured in Amesbury, this McCurd bus covered the Amesbury to Salisbury route for a number of years; it was the sixth vehicle to be put into service by the new firm. The first five were made at the Scout Motor Works in Salisbury, this one, however, was assembled at Hayes in Middlesex. The six machines, IB-801 to IB-806, were registered by Armagh County Council. This was, apparently, the only authority prepared to issue the Wilts. & Dorset concern with consecutive numbers which could be allocated to vehicles entering service at different times over a period of several weeks. We have been unable to identify the people in our picture; do you know who they are?

AMESBURY UNDER WATER in 1915. Taken in Countess Road, this photograph shows an army Studebaker staff car being recovered by two strong horses. Much of south Wiltshire was affected, particularly in and around Salisbury where some streets were under fourteen inches of water.

AMESBURY UNDER SNOW in April 1917. The heaviest snow fall since the record storm of 25 April 1908. Turn back a few pages and compare this view of the High Street with the one reproduced on page 21.

AMESBURY CARNIVAL CAPERS, in the 1920s. The happy youngsters pictured on the back of Harry Barnes' decorated cart are wearing Girl Guide and Cub uniforms. Tom Corp, Phyllis Eyres, Rupert Eyres, Roy Godfray, Eddie Tait and Phillip Thomas are among them. Carnivals were held annually in the Recreation Field or in the grounds of Amesbury Abbey. Usually they would take place on the nearest Saturday to the summer solstice but on one or two odd occasions the carnival was held on a Wednesday.

HOSPITAL CARNIVAL WEEK, June 1930. For the benefit of the new Ear, Nose and Throat Department at Salisbury Infirmary. The float depicted above was entered by the Amesbury Little Theatre. The theme was 'Shiraz, a mystic film of the East', which was showing at the Amesbury cinema. Ivor Buckland, Ernie Cockle and Laurie Marles are among the lads on the back of the lorry.

SALISBURY STREET AFTER THE RAIN, 11 July 1935. The Morris motor car can be seen moving slowly past Mrs Dyke's Tea Rooms and the garage of H. Norman Pitt & Co.

CHERRY'S WORLD RECORD, Easter 1939. Nine-year-old Cherry was the world's first non-pedigree Shorthorn cow to give more than 33,300 pints of milk in 365 days. The milk weighed a staggering 18 tons 10 cwt and 20 lbs, more than 30 times her own weight. She was milked four times daily, at 5 a.m., 11 a.m., 5 p.m., and 11 p.m., giving an average daily yield of eleven gallons and three pints. The photograph was taken at Wort and Way's Redhouse Farm (the site of the present police station).

AMESBURY TOWN BAND AT THE ABBEY MANSION, before the Second World War. Sir Cosmo Antrobus (wearing a cap) has Frederick George Cooper to his left (our right). Bandsman Southey can be seen to the left in the front row and Bandsman Worsdell to the right.

IVOR BUCKLAND AND HIS BLUE BOHEMIANS. The six musicians featured here were members of the band for around fifteen years from the time of its formation in the mid-1920s until they split up just before World War Two. Fred Mitchenall (bass), Leslie Hunt (trumpet), Ivor Buckland (saxophone), Ernie Cockle (piano), Jack Weston (drums) and Alec Milton (clarinet).

THE AMESBURY WOODBINES in 1920. Standing, left to right: Tom Worsdell, Fred Eyres, Bert Blake, Jack Baker, Frank Worsdell, Stan Hoslett, Alec Southey and Harold Ware. From the left, in the front row: R. Dibben, Fred Penny, William Cooper, Robert 'Bert' Rattue and B. White.

THE TEDWORTH HOUNDS MEET AT AMESBURY, in around 1907. Taken within the grounds of Abbey Park, Kent House can be seen to the right. Out of the picture to the left is Countess Road. Captain W.V. Faber was Master of Tedworth Hounds for many years.

THE MOTOR FIRE-ENGINE, *ANTROBUS*, at around the time of the Second World War. David Sloan is pictured driving the Merryweather appliance very slowly along Salisbury Street. On board, covered by the Union Jack, is a coffin containing the body of Fireman William Kirby who lived at Avon Buildings. He was a popular member of the Amesbury Town Band and a well-known character in the village. We believe that the fireman on the extreme right is 'A.B.' Willis. The *Antrobus* was delivered by train to Newton Toney Station in August 1911.

THE AMESBURY AMIABLES, *Stuck in the Lift*, in 1929. It is believed that the The Amesbury Amiables concert party was formed in around 1925 by Charles Williams. The players seen in this production are John Batsford as the lift attendant, Kathleen Pethen as the lady, the dressmaker's girl is played by Roselle Godfray (later Mrs Jones), the gentleman and ladies' escort is Mr Johnson (a bank manager) and the labourer is played by John Attwater.

WALKING QUICKLY INTO THE NEXT SECTION. A road race organized by Wilts. & Dorset Motor Services. More details on the next page.

The Durnfords, Netton, The Woodfords, Lake, Wilsford and West Amesbury.

THE AMESBURY TO SALISBURY ROAD RACE in 1939. Our picture, taken on the A345 at White Railings, shows Alan Toomer way ahead of his competitors. Employed by Wilts. & Dorset Motor Services as an apprentice electrician, Alan held his lead and won the Junior Cup.

MAD JACK'S MISHAP, 25 November 1912. The driver of this Foden traction engine, owned by W.E. Chivers & Sons of Devizes, was an impatient fellow. Wanting to gain speed while trundling slowly past White Railings he slipped the machine out of gear and as the pace increased the Foden started to wander violently from one side of the road to the other. Jack soon lost control, the wagon turned over and rolled down the bank. Rumour has it that he leapt from the machine, ran off and was never seen again.

HIGH POST FILLING STATION, after the Second World War. At the time of our photograph a gallon of Cleveland motor spirit was priced at 1s. 5d. Before 1960 the business was being managed by Major F. Weaver.

HIGH POST AERODROME HOTEL in 1946. The control tower of The Wiltshire School of Flying can clearly be seen. This private airfield was opened in 1931 by the Wiltshire Light Aeroplane and Country Club. During the Second World War, however, the airfield was being employed by Vickers Supermarine, Spitfire manufacturers.

THE MANOR HOUSE, GREAT DURNFORD, in 1907. Taken from a picture postcard addressed to Mrs Cornwell of Burson Terrace, Knowles Road, Gloucester: 'Dear Mother, We came down here on Monday, it is so pretty. In such a muddle, it will be nice when we are straight. What do you think of our house? Love to all, Rose.'

A FEW YEARS LATER. At this time, the property and residence of Captain Tryon. His chauffeur was probably preparing the Daimler laudaulette for a trip out, the hood is down and two trunks had been placed on the luggage rack. It can be seen that an extension has been added to the left side of the mansion.

THE CHURCH OF ST ANDREW, Durnford, before 1909. In 1883 the open seats and pulpit were renovated at the sole expense of Thomas Staples of Alderbury. Further repairs were carried out twenty years later at a cost of around £1,200 and a year after that, in 1904, five bells were rehung in the tower. The vicar during this period was the Revd Leicester Selby.

REVEREND ROBERT CHATFIELD, March 1864. Joint founder of the Durnford, Wilsford and Woodford Friendly Benefit Society which was instituted on 10 July 1833. Fellow officers of the society were George Dyer of the Court House, Edmund Olding (treasurer) of Woodford Mill and James Giles (secretary). Meetings were held at Woodford School Room.

THE POST OFFICE, GREAT DURNFORD, in 1907. John Newman was sub-postmaster at this time. His customers would mount their horses from the mounting block in front of the building. See if you can spot it next time you are passing by. The sign of the Black Horse Inn can be seen in the distance.

DURNFORD WATERMILL, before 1903. Christopher and Stephen Smith were milling here during the 1850s but by 1883 William Thorne was the registered keeper. Now known as Kingfisher Mill, this is the home of the Hon. Aylmer Tryon.

NETTON IN THE MID-TWENTIES. The trees in the distance are much taller now. Those which can be seen to the left, however, have gone and modern houses and bungalows have been built here. The dwelling to the right is Cobweb Cottage; this was a farm worker's cottage at the time of this photograph.

NETTON WESLEYAN CHAPEL, during the 1920s. Opened in 1895, this chapel is now a private dwelling. An extension has been added and it is pleasing to see that a plaque, similar to the one on the chapel, has been fixed there showing the date of its construction, 1989.

THORNTON'S NETTON BAKERY, established by Robert Thornton in 1833. In this photograph, which dates from the late 1890s, we can see Robert Thornton and a young man who is thought to be one of his six sons. They are pictured with the firm's two-wheeled delivery cart.

Left:
EDWARD 'TED' THORNTON is the man to the left of this 1920s photograph. Tom is harnessed to the four-wheeled baker's cart. We have not established the identity of the young man, however. Do you recognize him? The left-hand side of this building (part of the original bakery) is now Flint Cottage and the right-hand side is a private residence known as The Old Bakery. A modern house has been built on the land previously occupied by the bakery stables, this is now the home of Carolyn, the founder's great-great-granddaughter.

ROBERT AND ELIZA THORNTON. Robert, who was born at Amesbury in 1858, died in his ninetieth year. His wife Eliza was born in 1857 at Netton. The daughter of Robert and Maria (née Webb) Thornton, she passed away in 1943. This portrait photograph was taken in the studio of Bertram Mullins at 80 Castle Street, Salisbury towards the end of the twenties.

THORNTON'S A-TYPE FORD VAN, delivered in the autumn of 1928. The chassis, which came directly from the Ford factory, was sent to Acton's coachworks in Greencroft Street, Salisbury where this smart oak-framed van body was fitted. Taken near the old blacksmith's shop at Upper Woodford, our photograph shows Edward Thornton to the left and Valentine 'Val' Stokes.

'BY GRACE YE ARE SAVED'. The Netton Band of Hope was associated to the Wesleyan Chapel (see page 41). Throughout the early years of this century outdoor meetings were held on a regular basis in farmer Pile's field. Temperance groups from neighbouring districts were always invited, the Bourne Valley villages were often well represented.

SARAH TINHAM AND CHILDREN at Salterton. Arthur Tinham, a carpenter, was Sarah's husband and father to these lovely children. Elsie is pictured to the left, then Bert, Sarah (died in 1923 aged 66), Amy, Sydney and Ernest. They lived in White Cottage.

LITTLE DURNFORD HOUSE, before the First World War. The residence of Matthew H.W. Devenish JP. If you would like to see more old pictures of Durnford it is suggested that you search for a copy of Dorothy Devenish's delightful book, *A Wiltshire Home*, published in 1948.

THE BAYS AT LITTLE DURNFORD. The home of Walter and Lucy Uphill for ten years from around 1938/9. Chickens, ducks, geese and turkeys were kept, along with a goat who produced milk and a five-acre smallholding where vegetables were grown. Walter often sold his produce at Knapman, Lawes and Bament's yard in the Canal, Salisbury.

THE WHEATSHEAF AT LOWER WOODFORD, from a mid-twenties photographic postcard. In 1927 Edwin Davis Dear (the licensee) sent this postcard to Hardy and Sons of Salisbury suggesting that their traveller should phone him before calling to take an order. 'Our telephone number is Woodford 3'.

ISAAC HAZZARD'S LOWER WOODFORD GROCERY SHOP. Well established by the late 1920s, this small business continued to be listed in trade directories until 1947. The building is now a private residence which can be found opposite the entrance to Lower Woodford Manor.

THE WOODFORD BLACKSMITH, just after the Second World War. Leonard Moody was a blacksmith from the age of eighteen until his retirement in around 1964; his apprenticeship was served on the Broadlands Estate at Romsey. He loved football and was also a keen gardener and exhibitor at Woodford flower shows where he won many prizes.

ELSIE MOODY AND FOUR OF HER CHILDREN, in around 1917. Elsie (née Tinham) and Leonard brought up nine children, three boys and six girls. They were all born at Anvil Cottage in Middle Woodford. Dorothy, who at the present time resides at Anvil Cottage, is standing on the seat behind Arthur. Beatrice 'Betty' is on mum's knee and Sarah can be seen to the right. By turning back to page 45 you can catch a glimpse of Elsie as a child, holding her favourite doll when she was photographed with her family at Salterton.

GEORGE, BLANCH, HAROLD AND REG. Taken outside the kitchen window at the back of the Middle Woodford Post Office in 1911. William 'George' Dear can be seen standing behind his eldest son, Harold, and Blanch (née Portnall) is sitting with their youngest son Reginald on her knee.

MIDDLE WOODFORD POST OFFICE in 1907. The only money-order and telegraph office in the Woodford Valley. Pillar-boxes at Lower Woodford and Upper Woodford were cleared at 12 noon and 7.55 p.m. on weekdays and at 5.25 p.m. on Sundays.

WOODFORD ELEMENTARY SCHOOL in 1908. Built in 1872 to provide education for a maximum of one hundred children, the average attendance at this time was fifty. Mrs Emma Grasse was headmistress. This is now the Woodford Church of England Primary School.

THE WOODFORD SCHOOL PRESS in 1927. Pictured with their Adana printing press and plenty of lead type are the pupils responsible for producing the school magazine. Left to right: Wilfred Luffman, Ron Benson, Charlie Blake, Les Portnall, Fred West (sub-editor) and Charlie Benstead. Gilbert Portnall was editor.

THE MIDDLE WOODFORD CARPENTER'S SHOP, early this century. Edwin 'Arthur' Tinham stands, saw in hand, next to his apprentice who we believe to be Harry Gee. All kinds of things were made here, including coffins and cornices, trestles and trunks. Several sturdy pieces of oak furniture survive in the area. This is now a private dwelling known as The Old Workshop.

WOODFORD VILLAGE CLUB, pictured here in the early 1920s. Built in 1901, this community room was a gift to the people of the village from the Hon. Louis George Greville of Heale House, Lord of the Manor and principal landowner.

THE LORD OF THE MANOR'S MOTOR CAR AND CHAUFFEUR. This green Belsize landaulette was purchased by the Hon. Louis Greville in 1908. Alfred Chapel is pictured with the car outside the carriage sheds at Heale House. He started working here in 1900 as a groom but was soon made up to chauffeur.

THE CARPENTER'S SHOP AT UPPER WOODFORD, in around 1895. William Harding, the proprietor, can be seen in the middle of the picture and his eldest son, Harry, is to the left. Elsie (youngest) and Annie are sitting on the trestle and William junior is next to the pony.

FRANK MARCHANT ON HIS NEW-HUDSON MOTOR CYCLE. Frank, the son of Woodford blacksmith, Charlie Marchant, is pictured here at the back of his cottage in Upper Woodford (now known as Keeper's Cottage). The machine carries a Portsmouth registration, BK 3192.

STRAW BEE SKEPS AT UPPER WOODFORD in 1895. Taken opposite the Bridge Inn, this photograph shows William Conduit and his son Tom. William was a blacksmith and licensee of the Bridge. A very potent mead was made from the fermented honey and many a glass was enjoyed by the locals after a hard day's work in the fields.

THE BRIDGE INN in 1910. Viewed from the left: Mr West (first name unknown), Albert West, Miss Dolly Conduit (landlord's sister-in-law), Ted Green, Mrs Bessy Nobbs (wife of licensee), Miss Beatrice Phillips (later Mrs West), Harry Green and an unidentified person.

THE WEST FAMILY in 1921. Charles 'Charlie' West (born 1885), his wife Beatrice (née Phillips) and their only son Frederick 'Fred'. Charlie spent all his working life as a farm labourer at Heale. Fred (born in 1914) followed in father's furrows and spent twelve years working on the land for the Hon. Louis Greville. They are pictured here outside the home of the village blacksmith (now Keeper's Cottage). Sadly, Fred died just a few days after meeting the author, but thankfully there was time enough to record some of his memories of the Woodford Valley in days long gone.

THE HOME OF THE WEST FAMILY, 48 Upper Woodford. Beatrice is standing at the front door and we can see Fred's hoop and stick hanging to the right. Many years ago the district nurse lived in the cottage to the left of our picture.

LAKE HOUSE SOON AFTER ITS RESTORATION in 1898. Built in the seventeenth century, this was the property of Joseph William Lovibond, Lord of the Manor. He was also Chairman of Joseph Lovibond & Sons Ltd of Greenwich, Fulham, Salisbury and Bristol, and Chairman of Tintometer Ltd of Salisbury. The house was destroyed by fire on Good Friday, 1912.

THE DAY AFTER THE FIRE. This picture vividly illustrates the destructive force of the fire; the interior was totally devastated and only parts of the outer walls remain. Although the Volunteer Fire Brigades from Amesbury and Salisbury were commended for their actions they had been fighting a lost cause. The house was later rebuilt.

LAKE POST OFFICE AND COTTAGES in 1907. Now a single residence known as Post Office Cottage, at the time of this picture three families were living here. The most distant one was occupied in more recent times by District Nurse Lodge.

CARRYING THE ROYAL MAIL THROUGH LAKE, before the First World War. Many of the village mail carts were leased from William Henry Baker of St Paul's Road, Salisbury. He stabled the animals, garaged the vehicles and provided lodgings for the postmen.

THE STONEHENGE WOOLLEN INDUSTRY at Lake, in around 1906. The small thatched workshop in the background is now Fir Tree Cottage. This hamlet has suffered more than its fair share of fires; the cottages which appear to the right were burnt to the ground some years later.

THE NEW COTTAGES which replaced the ones shown in the upper picture. These in turn were destroyed during an outbreak of fire at around the time of the First World War. The well-constructed homes that stand on this site today are known as Diamond Cottages.

WILSFORD ELEMENTARY SCHOOL in 1903. Built in 1858 to accommodate forty children, the average attendance at this time, however, was just twenty-five. Miss Ellen Russell and all her pupils stand quite still for a few moments while photographer Charlie May of Gomeldon Hill, Porton, records their likeness.

WEST AMESBURY in 1904. The women are having a natter outside the residence known today as Merion Cottage. In the distance we can see West Amesbury House, the home of Frederick Turner.

Stonehenge, Orcheston, Shrewton and Winterbourne Stoke

A GIFT TO THE NATION. On 26 October 1918 Cecil Chubb presented to the nation one of the world's most famous monuments, Stonehenge. Mr Chubb (1876–1934), chairman of a private Salisbury hospital, succesfully bid for this prehistoric pile at a Salisbury auction in September 1915.

STONEHENGE CAFÉ during the 1930s, situated on the north side of the A360 near to its junction with the A303. The proprietor, Clement G. Billett, resided at Watergate, Countess Road, Amesbury.

AN OUTING TO THE STONES, at around the time of the First World War. These young men are believed to be members of Salisbury Swimming Club. The chap on the right of the back row is amateur photographer Charles Bridle; his favourite sport was water polo.

THE KING AT STONEHENGE. His Majesty King George V visited Salisbury Plain on several occasions during the First World War. At different times, mostly accompanied by Lord Kitchener, the king inspected troops encamped at Larkhill, Ludgershall, Tidworth and Warminster.

THE TURNSTILES AT STONEHENGE in the late-twenties. When visitors queued to pay their entrance fee they had the opportunity to buy postcards from the display on the side of the hut. Many of the views, including the one reproduced at the top of this page, were produced by Thomas Fuller of Amesbury.

THE DEDICATION OF THE MEMORIAL AT AIRMAN'S CORNER. On 5 July 1912 Captain E.B. Lorraine RE and Staff-Sergeant R.H.V. Wilson were killed when their Nieuport monoplane crashed near the crossroads on the Stonehenge to Shrewton Road. A picture of Captain Lorraine's funeral can be seen on page 96.

HUT BUILDING AT ROLLESTONE CAMP. The construction programme was well-advanced when a series of photographic postcards was produced in 1915. Bill Kilford of Shrewton left a note on the back of this one: 'I am working with men from all over the country.'

THE BUSTARD HOTEL, in around 1911. Landlord William Young frequently entertained the gentlemen of the press who lodged here while reporting on the movements of the troops encamped on Salisbury Plain.

ORCHESTON ST MARY in 1906. The ivy-covered cottage to the left has survived and is known as Sunnyside. The thatched ones in the middle of the picture, however, have gone. Replaced by a modern building, they were known to the locals as Warner's Cottages.

THE CROWN INN AT ORCHESTON, in around 1903. The board which can be seen on the side of the hostelry informs us that John Hall was the licensee at this time. A few years earlier Thomas Smith was the only registered beer retailer in the village.

FOSTER'S SMASH. Some time during the earlier 1920s Lady Torrington's Guy horsebox was being driven by Foster Carter. Although not entirely fruitless, our investigations have failed to resolve the mysteries of where, when, and how this accident occurred. Do you know the details?

LADY TORRINGTON ON A BRISTOL BIPLANE. This photograph was taken near the Bristol & Colonial Aeroplane Company's hangars at Larkhill in 1912. Viscountess Torrington resided at Elston House, Orcheston St George.

LONDON ROAD, SHREWTON, in 1904. Sundial Cottage can be seen to the left and the George Inn to the right. Henry Ackerman was keeper of the inn when this photograph was taken. A few months earlier, however, William Morrell was the licensee.

SUNDIAL COTTAGE in around 1908. The sundial, which is dated 1832, displays the motto, 'Life's but a walking shadow'. At different times, the Lovelock and Pitt families lived here.

OFF TO THE MATCH AT SWINDON TOWN. Pictured outside the Plume of Feathers on 10 January 1914, these Shrewton football supporters were just leaving for the north of the county to watch Swindon play Manchester United. The home team won 1–0. The Scout charabanc was made in Salisbury for John Hall & Son of Orcheston St George.

A HEARTY SEND-OFF, 5 August 1915. The people of Shrewton turned out in large numbers to say goodbye to three local lads who were departing to join Kitchener's army. Steve Jukes is at the wheel of this Model T Ford, and George Smith is sitting behind him. We do not know the names of the other two. They are seen here in the Plume of Feathers' yard.

THE SHREWTON NEWSAGENT in the early twenties. The hut was situated in the Plume of Feathers' yard. Publican James Bundy can be seen to the left, Jack 'Speedy' Carter is in the middle, and Mr Bundy's son Herbert is to the right. The name painted on the tradebike indicates that this was Herbert's business.

UNFURLING THE FLAG, 23 September 1908. Spirits were high despite the weather on the day the Earl of Radnor unfurled the new flag and presented cups to the best rifle shots at Shrewton School. A large number of people turned out to witness the event but only around half of them can be seen in our photograph.

GALLOPING HORSES TO THE SOUND OF A GAVIOLI in 1909. For many years the people of Shrewton celebrated Trinity Monday. They were busy days; the local friendly societies met at the fair field in the morning and in the afternoon the children were entertained to tea. The thrills and spills were provided by Henry Jennings of Devizes.

AN EXCURSION TO THE PRIORY CHURCH OF EDINGTON, in the early 1920s. The first vehicle is Edwin Withers' Leyland coal lorry (thoroughly cleaned for the occasion), followed by one of John Hall's saloon buses and to complete the convoy, Mr Sainsbury's Overland carrier's van. Reverend Bull, Dolly Gant and Ina Kilford are just three of the people who have been identified in this group.

THE PEARCE FAMILY, photographed at Pampas Villas, Maddington in around 1890, now known as the White House. Joseph John Smart Pearce is standing at the back to the right of his sons, Joseph Samuel (1865–1932) and Wilfred John (1878–1967). Joseph's mother, Sabina Frances Game Pearce (née Smart), is sitting to the left and his wife Ann (née White) is to the right. The three young ladies are Ann's daughters; Caroline Elizabeth, Sabina Frances and Winifred Annie. Our photograph was copied from an original which hangs in the Shrewton home of Janet Hall, the granddaughter of Wilfred John Pearce.

A VIEW FROM PAMPAS VILLA, taken at around the same time as the group photograph on the opposite page. Ann Pearce can be seen to the left, Wilfred John is standing by the pony and Sabina Frances is sitting in the trap. This field was often the venue for coronation teas, jubilees, club days, fairs, fêtes and Trinity Monday gatherings.

A VIEW ALONG MADDINGTON in 1909. The cart was owned by the Chant family who were bakers and grocers in Shrewton for many years. Flood Cottages can be seen on the right, nearest to the camera, followed by Pampas Villa and in the distance the dwellings now known as Park View.

A BRISTOL BIPLANE LANDED NEAR THE GIBBET in around 1910. Inquisitive spectators arrived from all around the district to catch a glimpse of this wonderful flying machine. Many of these country folk would have heard the aeroplanes and perhaps caught sight of one in the distance, but it was a rare opportunity to actually touch one.

PULLING UP THE SPUDS in 1924. These two heavy chestnut horses can be seen pulling a potato spinner across a field on Wort and Way's Shrewton farm. Pictured left to right are: Johnny Leonard, Bill Ingram, Jack Cooper, Tommy Miller and Reg 'Johner' Sainsbury.

SHREWTON CLUB FÊTE in 1909, organized by the local friendly benefit societies and held in a field at Maddington. The 'Safe and Up-to-Date' galloping horses ride in the background was supplied by Henry Jennings of Devizes. Just behind the swinging boats we can see a luxurious living van and the steam traction engine which generated the electricity to power the rides.

CANADIAN TROOPS AT THE OLD VILLAGE LOCK-UP. In October 1914 Canadian and Newfoundland divisions moved into camps at Bustard, West Down (North and South) and Pond Farm. A note on the back of this photograph states that 'We are camped at Shrewton'. The steam tractor which can be seen over the bridge was in service with 63rd Company Army Service Corps, Bulford and was probably used to haul heavy guns.

A SNAP TO SEND HOME TO THE FAMILY. Shrewton photographers Albert Marett and Walter 'Bill' Ross were kept very busy during the early years of this century. In January 1915 they took many snaps of both local people and soldiers who were up to their knees in flood water. This group are pictured near Izaac Collins' Catharine Wheel public house.

A BIZARRE BAZAAR IN THE HIGH STREET, 1905. The women nearest to the camera are standing outside Elizabeth Cox's bazaar which is now a private house named Bizarre. The white-bearded man is at the door of the post office which was managed by Dennis Guyatt; this is now Bury View.

THE CHANT FAMILY. Rimmelion can be seen to the left with Albert on her knee. To her left, at the back, is Herbert, next comes Henry junior, then Henry, Alice, Willie and Ted. The four young ones in the front are Arthur, Lewis (between Henry's knees), Sidney and Millie. Henry Chant founded a grocery and bakery business in around 1870.

DOLLY CHANT AND 'TIN LIZZY'. Pictured here in the twenties with one of the firm's Model T Ford vans is Herbert Chant's daughter, Dolly. Although AA 8667 was registered in Hampshire it was more common for the firm's delivery vehicles to display Wiltshire plates. One example of this is AM 5383 which can just be seen in the shed in the background.

ALBERT VICTOR CHANT, a Shrewton bandsman.

WINTERBOURNE STOKE during the First World War. Nearest to the camera is George Stanley Grant's Post Office and Grocery Store. This building was demolished some years later and the site is now occupied by the Stonehenge Filling Station. The houses and the Bell Inn, however, have survived.

A YEAR OR TWO LATER. Since the previous photograph was taken the business had been sold and a name board has appeared above the shop window: 'H.J. Lockyer. Baker, Grocer, Over-seer and Sub-postmaster.' The white 20 hp Model T Ford van (AM 4444), however, is still in the old livery of G.S. Grant.

'GRANDAD' BRICE, employed as a carter at Druid's Lodge Farm, pictured here in the early 1920s.

Larkhill, Durrington and Bulford

THE PACKWAY, LARKHILL, in the 1930s. With the exception of the army huts which can just be seen in the background, this scene looks very much the same today. The trees are much taller now and the old style telephone box has been replaced by two modern ones.

LARKHILL CAMP during the First World War. The construction of the iron and timber huts pictured here was completed by 1915. Before this time all units were accommodated under canvas. The work was carried out by civil engineering contractor Sir John Jackson.

AEROPLANE HANGARS AT LARKHILL erected for the Bristol and Colonial Aeroplane Company Limited in 1910. These buildings, which can still be seen in Wood Road, were used by the Bristol Flying School. A Bristol monoplane and Sir George White's Argyll motor car are parked outside the sheds.

THE STEAM LOCOMOTIVE *SALISBURY* was employed at Larkhill until 1918 when it was transferred to Longmore. Manufactured in 1914 by Hudswell & Clarke of Leeds, this engine (No. 1069) was purchased by Sir John Jackson Limited.

SAMUEL FRANKLIN CODY, aviator and inventor. Pictured here with the Cody biplane which won the military trials at Larkhill in August 1912. He received a £5,000 first prize and an order for one of his machines. He was killed after a tragic accident over Laffan's Plain on 7 August 1913 when the aeroplane that he was flying broke up while coming in to land.

THE STONEHENGE INN AT DURRINGTON, in around 1870 when William Herbert Toomer was the licensee. A contemporary advertisement states that the establishment was also a 'Brewery, Posting House, Livery and Bait Stables'. In November 1893 Herbert Corp purchased the freehold through auctioneer J.T. Woolley of Salisbury.

A THORNYCROFT BUS AT THE STONEHENGE INN, on the Wilts. & Dorset service through Amesbury to Salisbury. Bill Netton is the driver and his friend Jack Weston the conductor. The return fare was 2s. 6d. and a single 'Workingman's Ticket' was just 10d.

DURRINGTON STONES AND ALL SAINTS' CHURCH in 1899. The rector from 1863 to 1910 was Revd Charles Snelling Ruddle. His most memorable feature was his curly white beard which was a good 12 in long.

DURRINGTON HOSPITAL SUNDAY, 1907. Members of the Durrington Brass Band and around one hundred local people are gathered for an open air service. Similar events were organized in Bulford, Netheravon and Upavon. The Rectory, which can be seen in the background, was destroyed by fire on 19 October 1922.

THE POST OFFICE IN BULFORD ROAD, Durrington, before 1908. The vacant ground to the right of our picture was soon developed and an almost identical building was erected there. The dwelling in Bulford Road which is today called The Old Post Office is not the property which we can see in this photograph.

THE DURRINGTON BLACKSMITH in the mid-twenties. Mr Toomer can be seen here with his striker, Ben. The smithy was to be found almost opposite the post office and Attwater's Dairy which is shown in the upper picture.

A VICTORIAN VIEW OF DURRINGTON. Long since demolished, these pretty thatched cottages stood on land now occupied by the bungalows in College Lane. The photograph was taken in 1899 when the Climax Photo Company of London were touring the area.

JAMES MILNE'S CHEMIST AND PHARMACY in around 1912. The enterprise, situated on the corner of Bulford Road and Windsor Road, was short-lived. The business name appeared only twice in local trade directories, firstly in 1911 and again in 1914.

MARY, THE WIFE OF FRANK TOOMER, taken from a cabinet photograph of the early 1890s. There is just enough space here to feature two of Frank and Mary's eight children. Beatrice 'Beat' can be seen in the lower picture and Sam is depicted on the next page. Frank, a farmer, lived in the village from 1847 until his death in 1923. He was the first chairman of Durrington Parish Council.

MARY AND BEATRICE feeding calves in the orchard off College Lane. Mary was a very independent woman of strong character, she was keeper of her own accounts and an early believer in Women's Lib. Much to the wonderment of the congregation at All Saints', she frequently took her pet dog to church on Sundays. It was well-behaved and sat beside her in the pews.

SAM TOOMER WITH HIS SAFETY CYCLE. Another of the cabinet prints supplied by the Climax Photo Company after their photographer visited the area in 1899.

DURRINGTON GEISHA GIRLS in 1910. These pretty little ladies are believed to be taking part in a Durrington School concert. A number of other photographs of this event which have survived illustrate different themes. These include fairies, dunces, kings and queens.

DURRINGTON BRASS BAND AT WOODFORD FLOWER SHOW, 22 August 1906. The band made frequent visits to the villages in the Woodford Valley, many times to play at the Annual Flower Show, now and again to give a concert, and at least once to attend a funeral.

TOM CHAPMAN AT THE DOOR OF HIS DURRINGTON STORES, in around 1924. Tom managed the grocery and hardware departments to the right and his wife Bessie (née Maidment) traded from the left-hand unit. Situated in Bulford Road, this site is now occupied by new enterprises which include Fish 'N' Chips, A Cut Above and A. & R. News.

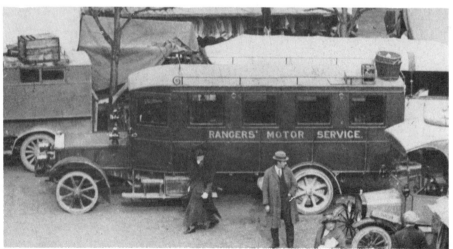

THE DURRINGTON CARRIER in Salisbury Market Place, March 1921. This Alldays and Onions saloon bus was operated for many years by Mark Ranger & Sons. A superior machine in its day, it sported many of the latest features, including electric lighting and cushioned seats in the passenger compartment.

WATER STREET, BULFORD, IN THE THIRTIES. This view has changed very little over the years and even the thatched cottages pictured here have survived. Although now past retiring age, these two people could still be living in the area. Are you one of them?

THE BULFORD AIR RAID WARDEN AND HIS WIFE. This picture of Emily and Percy Pearce was taken on 24 June 1941, on the occasion of their silver wedding anniversary. They lived at 214 High Street which was later renumbered 21. Emily and Percy can be seen here with Nelly their pet dog.

BULFORD HOSPITAL SUNDAY in 1907. This is the scene at Orchard End where villagers assembled before taking part in the procession. Bulford Post Office can be found here today. In the background we can see James Hooper's steam-ploughing engine and the Durrington Band. The large shed to the left is where Mr Hooper stored his farm machinery.

BULFORD TUG OF WAR TEAM, seen here in 1910 at Victoria Park, Salisbury. We do not know the names of all these men but we can say that William 'Bill' Symonds is the chap to the left wearing a black waistcoat. The tall fellows at the back are thought to be the Lake brothers.

A SCOUT CAR AT WATERGATE HOUSE, Bulford. Built at Messrs Burden Brothers and Radcliffe's motor works in Salisbury, this 24/28 hp, blue-painted tonneau was purchased by Allan Carruth Young in January 1910. Pictured behind the wheel of the car in 1913 is Mr Young's chauffeur, Harry Norman. In December 1916 the car was sold to Salisbury taxi-driver Herbert Mirfin.

EDWARD PEARCE, BULFORD DAIRYMAN. Mr Pearce was a busy chap; he managed a small dairy farm at Bulford, delivered milk regularly to households in and around Bulford and Durrington, and three times a week he operated a carrying service through Amesbury to Salisbury.

THE BULFORD CARRIER. Percy Pearce (Edward's son) is photographed with the horse-drawn van at Bulford Camp some time before the First World War. On Tuesday, Thursday and Saturday each week a round trip was made to Salisbury, calling at Bulford village, Bulford Camp, Durrington and Amesbury.

THE BULFORD VAN, just before World War One. This chain-driven Daimler can be seen outside The Chough in Blue Boar Row, Salisbury. We believe this to be the motor that Pearce's operated before 1918 after which time two Ford Model T vans were used.

THE FUNERAL OF CAPTAIN E.B. LORRAINE in 1912. The band is playing Beethoven's Funeral March as the cortège moves slowly in the direction of Bulford station. A picture of the dedication of Capt. Lorraine's Memorial can be seen on page 64.

DUNG CARTS AT BULFORD CAMP in the twenties. The large number of horses at the camp ensured that these men were kept very busy. We have identified three of them: Ron Sturgess, Mike Lacey and 'Scooty' Hunt. The Wesleyan Soldiers' Home can be seen in the right background.

BULFORD CAMP STABLES, during the First World War. Horses were by no means the only form of transport here. There were several units of the Army Service Corps who maintained a wide variety of military trucks, ambulances, staff cars and even a number of steam gun-tractors.

BULFORD TIN TOWN, after the First World War. Now known as Bond Street, this thoroughfare was the commercial centre of the camp. The following are some of the firms who were trading here at this time: Hobden Brothers (outfitters), Frederick Lawes (fruiterer), Lloyds Bank, Percy Mussell (hairdresser), W.H. Smith (newsagents), and photographer Harry Morse who took this picture.

THE REFRESHMENT BAR AT MISS PERK'S HOME, Bulford, before 1914. Built at a cost of £7,000 and established around the turn of the century, this home was open to all soldiers irrespective of their religious or other beliefs. The facilities included a restaurant, devotional rooms, recreation rooms, bedrooms and bathrooms. The building was located at Sling Plantation.

Figheldean, Netheravon, Enford, Chisenbury and Upavon

'THE FAMOUS MOTOR CHAPEL AT FIGHELDEAN in 1911.' This notation appears on the back of the original photograph. Several older residents of the village can recall that members of The Church Army toured the area twice every year in an effort to convert non-believers. This vehicle is a Hallford, built in Dartford.

FIGHELDEAN POST OFFICE, before 1920. Henry John Sheppard was the sub-postmaster at this time. Letters arrived from Salisbury at 6.10 a.m. and were delivered from 9.45 a.m. Monday to Saturday, and during the afternoon on Sundays.

CHURCH LANE, FIGHELDEAN, before 1917. This village was neglected by the early photographers of south Wiltshire and only a relatively small number of prints have survived. The majority of these were produced by Thomas Fuller of Amesbury but due to poor definition they have not been reproduced in this book.

A TALE OF TWO TERRIERS. In the right-hand corner of this 1916 view of Mill Lane, Figheldean, we can see a very old brown terrier named Moses. Most of the time, and much to the annoyance of his puppy friend Koko, he would lie sleeping in the lane. Koko was often to be seen running around his old chum whining and wagging his tail. Moses thought this was a total waste of energy and would just lie there and not take the slightest notice.

UNDER THE SPREADING CHESTNUT TREE. Since the first half of the last century this is where the Figheldean smithy was to be found. At around the time of the First World War, when this photograph was taken, Bernard Sheppard was working here. He was a farrier, general blacksmith and carrier and in later years, secretary of Figheldean Reading Room.

KING'S HILL, NETHERAVON, in around 1920. Charles Carter can just be seen standing in the doorway of his shop. By 1935 the business was under the management of Leopold Diamond, former associate of the Angel Hotel in Salisbury. The shop was closed a year or two ago and is now only being used as a store.

NURSE WALKER IN HER PONY AND TRAP. The Netheravon District Nursing Association (affiliated to the Queen Victoria Jubilee Nursing Institute) employed Nurse Walker soon after its formation in January 1881. Her conveyance was purchased towards the end of 1894 at a cost of £12 5s. 4d.

JOHN AND MARY ELLIOTT of Netheravon. This 1879 carte-de-visite photograph is taken from a remarkable collection of Victorian photographs and cuttings recently discovered in Christchurch, Dorset. In addition to portraits of people and buildings, the three albums contain images of many memorable events. These include a snowfall in 1881, the 1887 Golden Jubilee of Queen Victoria, numerous fêtes and festivals, and the coronation celebrations of 1902 and 1911.

NETHERAVON TOP HAT CLUB FÊTE, 1909. On 19 May the Netheravon Sickness Benefit Society was celebrating another successful year. In the morning the men of the village were served breakfast at the Dog and Gun Inn, and in the afternoon the children had lots of fun at Henry Jennings' fair.

THE NETHERAVON OTTER HUNT, between the wars. There was a good turn out on this particular day when the river was worked through Fittleton, Enford, Chisenbury, Upavon and Sharcott. Messrs Hussey, Saunders and Whitmarsh can be seen in this group.

A KITE FAMILY PORTRAIT in 1898. The little boy on the pony is Luther Clifford Kite, pictured here with his father Edwin who kept the orchard which now forms part of Orchard Farm. Do you recognize the two girls? Netheravon School Cottage can be seen in the right background.

HOSPITAL SUNDAY in 1909. Headed by the Figheldean brass band, the following bodies marched from Haxon Green to Netheravon Park: Netheravon Friendly Society, the Netheravon Branch of the Wiltshire Friendly Benefit Society, the Avon Court of the Ancient Order of Forresters and the Slate Clubs of Figheldean and Netheravon.

A LITTLE FLOWER GIRL. Dating from the early 1930s, this pleasing photograph shows Madge Hams (now Mrs Powell) and her mother Helen. Madge took part in a Netheravon carnival with her bicycle which was lavishly decorated with flowers, flags and bunting of many different colours. The cavalcade marched through the village to Samuel Gregory's field where Mr Jennings had set up his fairground rides.

NETHERAVON POLICE, during the Second World War. Can you find the faces that belong to these names? SC Baden-Powell, Sgt. Barlow, Mr Bradley, SC Carpenter, Harry Groom, SC Hayward, PC Nicholas, Frank Sawyer and Sgt. Webber-Taylor.

NETHERAVON 'WINGS FOR VICTORY', during the Second World War. With the exception of Mr J. Lamont (Tunisia), the national costumes of our allies are being modelled by ladies from the Netheravon branch of the WI and the Red Cross. They include Mrs Dryden, Maggie Oborne and Kate Phillimore. From the left in the front we can see, Peter Mead, Vic King, Ron Bailey, Ted Hitchcock (warden) and Percy Hams.

THE NETHERAVON CARRIER. For many years Alfred White ran a twice weekly motor service from Netheravon to Salisbury. He lived in the dwelling now known as Owl Cottage and his GMC van, pictured here in Castle Street, Salisbury in March 1921, was garaged next to the present day Spar shop.

LOWER AIRFIELD CAMP, Netheravon. This photograph was taken in 1913 when the huts were being built. The labourers employed on this construction project came from all over the country so you can understand why we have not identified these three workmen.

HAXON OR HAXTON BRIDGE, before the First World War. This painted iron bridge was dismantled many years ago and replaced with one built of brick. It is now known as Red Bridge.

A COUNCIL ROAD REPAIR GANG AT HAXON, before 1909. We believe that Sid Stephens was the driver of this Aveling and Porter steam-roller and Fred 'Middle 'un' Sheppard was the foreman. Neddy Hitchcock can be seen standing behind the wheel.

GROUP TWO AT FITTLETON SCHOOL, in around 1904. At the time of this photograph Mrs Sophia Capel was the headmistress of Fittleton Elementary School. She held the post from the mid-1890s until sometime before 1920 when Miss Dorothy Worsfold became principal. Established in 1735 to accommodate around 120 children, the building was extended in 1872 when an additional room was added. The average number of children attending during the year to December 1903 was just forty-nine. The school was supported in part by Mrs Buckenham's yearly endowment of £1 4s. In 1989 Enford, Fittleton, and Netheravon schools were amalgamated, and at the time of writing a new owner is being sought for the Fittleton Schoolhouse.

ENFORD POST OFFICE in around 1907. At least three people held the position of sub-postmaster between 1900 and the start of the First World War: John Bushell (1903), Joses Carter (1906/7) and James Nash (1910/12). Our picture is reproduced from a postcard published by W.J. Selfe of Market Place, Pewsey. A William J. Selfe was proprietor of a cycle shop in North Street, Pewsey, but it is uncertain whether this is the same person.

GEORGE PERRETT'S ENFORD BAKERY, after 1920. The bakers pictured here from the left are Walter Holmes, Bob Goodship and Percy Fay. Established before the First World War and situated in Long Street, this business survived until around twenty years ago. At one time an enamel sign on the bakehouse wall advertised Hovis bread with the slogan 'Crowned with the King's Approval'. The building is now a private dwelling known as The Old Bakery.

MISS CLARKE AND HER PUPILS at Enford School, in around 1925. Fred Elkins and Stanley Reddick can be seen here and at the time of writing they are both still living in the village. The first school at Enford was established in 1552 and the most recent one closed in 1989, a span of 437 years.

AN EDWARDIAN VIEW OF THE HILL, ENFORD. The children depicted here had probably never seen a photographer at work before. No doubt they were intrigued by what was going on under the black cloth after they had been asked to stand motionless for a few seconds.

CHISENBURY POST OFFICE AND STORES in 1909. Mary Weeks started trading here at around the turn of the century, although her name did not appear in local trade directories until a few years later. Her business was included in the Kelly's 1903 list of shopkeepers.

MRS WEEKS AND TED COX, pictured together outside Chisenbury Post Office and Stores on a sunny day between the First and Second World Wars. Before the post office was incorporated with the general store in 1906 there was only a letter-box situated here. This building is now a private house.

BRIDLE BRIDGE AT CHISENBURY in 1909. Hundreds of pictures depicting life in and around Upavon were produced by Whitfield Cosser of 3 High Street, Devizes from 1906 to 1909, and by his successor Horace Edmonds (at the same address) from 1909 until just before the Second World War. This is one of Mr Edmonds' pictures.

ANDOVER ROAD, UPAVON, in 1914. The Pewsey Motor Company was trading here at this time. The firm sold both new and used cars, carried out repairs and also let cars out on hire. In this photograph we can see a Ford Model T tourer (AA 4170) and a 14 hp dark blue Scout tonneau (AM 2148).

UPAVON POST OFFICE before October 1910, when Miss Selina F. King was the sub-postmistress. Our photograph was sent to Miss E.A. Bays of the Parish Room, Enford on 25 October 1910. A note was written on the back of it: 'Dear Miss Bays, This is a photograph of our house. Do you recognize it?' Signed, Nellie Woodford.

UPAVON HIGH STREET before 1908. Alfred Yeates' Antelope Inn can be seen to the left and Albert Porter's Drapery and Grocery Store to the extreme right. The Billiard Room which forms part of the Antelope Inn is presently being offered for sale as a suitable site for a two-bedroomed cottage.

UPAVON PRIMITIVE METHODIST SUNDAY SCHOOL OUTING, pictured at the Roebuck Inn, Salisbury *en route* for Bournemouth on 24 July 1922. This Dennis saloon bus was operated by Edwin Cave who can be seen at the front, just left of centre, with his children Ella and Alan. To Edwin's left is Sarah, the wife of James Mortimer who was the Upavon mail-cart driver.

UPAVON HOSPITAL SUNDAY in 1906. The procession which started at Frank Chisman's farm at Widdington can be seen here in Devizes Road. A local brass band took part, as well as numerous decorated carts and members of the Upavon Friendly Societies.

WIDDINGTON FARM IN THE TWENTIES. Vintage agricultural tractors and farm machines are much sought after these days by the enthusiasts who collect and restore them. Charlie Wiltshire can be seen to the left of our picture and we believe that the other chap is Ernest Yeates.

HEADING FOR THE LONDON MARKETS. For many years Charlie Andrews had the sole rights to catch rabbits in and around Upavon and on parts of Salisbury Plain. The ones loaded on this wagon were sent to London by train. Pictured left to right are: Charlie Wiltshire, Charlie Andrews, Herbert 'Farmer' Bailey and Charlie Pinchin.

THE SHIP INN at Upavon, before the First World War. Thomas Chamberlain was the proprietor of the butchers shop which can just be seen to the right. Several older residents of the village can remember the good deals they had when he returned from next door after enjoying a jug or two.

STREET ENTERTAINERS AT THE SHIP, in around 1910. Hubert Edgar 'Charlie' Andrews can be seen to the right (towel over shoulder and pint in hand). He was host at the Ship Inn from 1908 until sometime before 1920 when he moved across the road to manage the Antelope Inn. It was at this time that Moses Fagence became the landlord of the Ship.

Everleigh, Ludgershall, Tidworth, Shipton Bellinger and Cholderton.

THE CROWN HOTEL, EVERLEIGH, during the early 1920s. This 20 hp black-painted Model T Ford (HR 683) was owned by Joseph James 'J.J.' Hunt (proprietor of photographic studios in Calne, Ludgershall and Marlborough). We know that this is one of J.J.'s pictures but we have not been able to identify the young lady who is sitting in his car. Do you recognize her?

THE STREET, EVERLEIGH, before 1910, showing Albert Henry Howse's shop and post office. This building can still be seen but the thatched cottages beyond have long since been demolished. This is another of J.J.'s photographs.

VICKER'S SHOP AT LUDGERSHALL in 1911. Arthur C. Vicker was a butcher and baker for a short time before the First World War, trading from this unit at October House, High Street, Ludgershall. In more recent years a VG store was situated here and presently it is occupied by K.A. Gardner.

AN EDWARDIAN VIEW OF LUDGERSHALL. Yates' Stores is now Lloyds Bank and the Halifax Building Society. By the turn of the century Arthur Edward Yates was trading here as a grocer, provision dealer, baker, draper, ironmonger and a dealer in tobaccos.

YATES' STEAM DELIVERY VAN. Built before 1914 by W. Tasker & Sons of Waterloo Ironworks, Anna Valley, near Andover. The wagon was used to transport goods to the many military camps that were dotted around Salisbury Plain. This heavy monster has wooden wheels and solid rubber tyres.

THE KING'S MEN AT LUDGERSHALL RAILWAY STATION. A division of the North Somerset Yeomanry had arrived here in 1909 on the last leg of their journey to Perham Down Camp. George Humphries was station master at this time.

THE RAM INN AT TIDWORTH in 1906. Originally part of the Tedworth Estate, this hostelry was purchased by the War Office in September 1897, along with 13 farms, 8 farmhouses and 107 cottages (6,618 acres in all). In January 1920 it was sold to Portsmouth United Breweries, after which time it was rebuilt.

NORTH TIDWORTH POST OFFICE in 1907. This enterprise was not the sole interest of Edwin Eyles; he managed a grocery store, a drapers shop, and a horse-drawn carrier service to Salisbury every Tuesday and to Andover on Wednesdays and Fridays. In more recent times this has been a newsagents and a fancy goods shop.

GARRISON AND DISTRICT MOTORS in 1925, situated in Station Road, South Tidworth. The display board advertises 'The Latest fleet of Chars-a-bancs in the District, All on Pneumatic-tyres. Any make of car supplied. Hire Purchase terms arranged'. The chemists shop which can be seen to the right was managed by Percy Cheetham.

TIDWORTH GARRISON, at around the time of the First World War. By 1905 the War Department had built eight blocks of barracks on land purchased from John William Kelt in 1897. There were four cavalry barracks, Aliwal, Assaye, Candahar and Mooltan; and four infantry barracks, Bhurtpore, Delhi, Jellalabad and Lucknow.

HIGH STREET, SHIPTON BELLINGER, in around 1907. With the exception of Shipton Bellinger and South Tidworth all the villages portrayed here are in Wiltshire. A recent quote by Sam Hart – 'It has been Salisbury to which villagers have traditionally gone for commerce and markets' – suggests that these two Hampshire villages are not out of place in this book.

THE HANTS. AND WILTS. LAUNDRY at Shipton in 1915. A multitude of woollen blankets are piled up near the boiler house. These were collected from local military camps. After being washed the clean blankets were hung out to dry on row upon row of clothes lines that were erected in the fields behind the laundry.

THE PLANK FAMILY. Bert is standing on the extreme left next to his sister Hilda, then comes Harry (the eldest son), Fred, and Len who is still living in the village. Gladys and Jessie are sitting in front of their father, Stan, who is pictured here with Elsie on his lap. Kate is the mother of these children and she is sitting next to John.

SHIPTON CASH STORES, situated in High Street, Shipton Bellinger, and established at around the turn of the century. F.W. Harrison was the proprietor, and we can tell from the photograph above that his was a multi-faceted business: a draper, outfitter, baker, grocer and provisions merchant. The three young men pictured with the firm's horse-drawn delivery van were bakers, their names are Bradbury, Waite and Gale.

PERRIORS AND THE FLOOD in January 1915. The man standing in the middle of the photograph below is Albert Perrior, the Shipton blacksmith. His thatched cottage (now Forge Cottage) and the smithy are to be seen in the background. The delivery cart is the same as the one shown on the opposite page. In the photograph to the right, taken in front of Forge Cottage, we can see Albert 'Grandad' Perrior, his wife May and their son Arthur and daughter Mary.

BULFORD ROAD, SHIPTON BELLINGER, before 1913. The tall house in the distance has survived and is known today as Riverside. The cottages nearest to the camera, however, have gone and several bungalows have replaced them. The horse-drawn cart was employed by Shipton Supply Stores.

HENRY CHARLES 'INKY' STEPHENS (1841–1918). The son of Dr Henry Stephens, inventor of the famous blue-black writing fluid. Several generations of the Stephens family have lived in the area. Henry Charles is buried in the grounds of St Nicholas' church at Cholderton.

CHOLDERTON STORES AND POST OFFICE in 1907, now a private residence. James Jenkinson was shopkeeper and sub-postmaster here from before the turn of the century until just before the Second World War. An entry in a 1939 trade directory names the sub-postmaster as Wilfred Jenkinson. Could this be James' son?

'GOING HOME.' Taken during the floods of January 1915 this captioned photograph was discovered a few years ago in the larder at Wilbury Farm House. Found to be in a very poor state, the print has since been repaired and retouched by the author. The timber wagon depicted here has just passed the white fences which lead to Cholderton House.

CHURCH LANE, CHOLDERTON, in 1908, with the church of St Nicholas in the background. The dwellings known today as Tharfield Cottage and St Nicholas Cottage are still thatched, the ivy-clad unit nearest to the camera, however, now has a slated roof. Do you recognize the postman or the soldier?

TAKE FIVE. The two carts, pictured here in 1908, are parked beside the bridge that leads to Charles Bundy's hostelry, the Crown Inn at Cholderton. There are no prizes on offer to those who correctly guess where the carters could be found. Mr Bundy was also a farmer and haulier.

Newton Toney, Allington, Boscombe and Idmiston

THE TEDWORTH HOUNDS AT WILBURY HOUSE, the residence of Captain Harry Charles Malet. Our photograph shows the opening meet of the season. During the 1920s the pack hunted every Tuesday, Thursday and Saturday. Lt.-Col. F.W.L. Cavendish was the master.

A COMMITTEE MEETING AT WILBURY HOUSE. Many of these gentlemen are wearing a 'committee' badge but we have no idea what they were organizing; do you know? We have identified a few of them: Major James Despencer-Robertson (Salisbury MP), John Young senior, John Rowland Hoare (Allington baker) and Mr Curtis (Allington farmer).

NEWTON TONEY, at around the time of the First World War. The children can be seen playing near the village post office where George Brown was sub-postmaster. The sign above the door to the left reads, 'George Brown. Butcher. Licensed dealer in Tea and Tobacco.'

THE MALET ARMS AT NEWTON TONEY in around 1904, when Mrs Martha Olden was the host. The inn was named after a former lord of the manor who lived at Wilbury House.

WATER, WATER, EVERYWHERE! Newton Toney, like many other south-Wiltshire towns and villages, did not escape the severe floods of January 1915. Pictured here in the waters around the Malet Arms is the horse-drawn tilt which John Rowland Hoare of Allington used to deliver his bread.

THE NEWTON TONEY BUS, before the Second World War. The man who can be seen in our picture is the owner/driver, Harold Armstead. A return service to Salisbury was operated on Tuesday, Thursday and Saturday each week. The conveyance (MR 3418) was based on an 18 hp Guy 25 cwt chassis to which a blue-painted body with fourteen seats was fitted. The livery changed later to silver grey and black.

NEWTON TONEY RAILWAY STATION, on the branch-line which ran from the main Salisbury–Andover line of the London & South Western Railway to Amesbury. The man in the centre of the picture we believe to be Charles Leach the station master. Here the alternative spelling of the village's name is seen on the station sign.

TRINITY MONDAY AT NEWTON TONEY in 1912. Taken by Henry Buckle, this photograph shows the villagers in their Sunday best. The little girl in the centre of the group is Nelly Steele (now Mrs Allen), pictured here with her mother, Martha, and brothers, Arthur and Ernest. Later in the day the children were served tea at the school.

THE NEWTON TONEY BAND OF HOPE, on the occasion of the annual Bourne Valley Temperance Movement rally. The Newton Toney contingent, seen here with a local Salvation Army band, had travelled to Mr Pile's field at Netton on farm wagons which had been loaned for the day by White Brothers. The year is 1911.

EMMA, BEATRICE, JOHN AND KITTY. Taken outside Chapel Cottage at Allington during the First World War, our picture shows John and Emma Young with their daughter-in-law, Beatrice, and Kitty the pony. John was a farm bailiff to William Q. Cole.

HARRY 'JOHN' YOUNG (1894–1979). For a number of years, while employed as a gamekeeper by Major James Despencer-Robertson, John lived in one of the lodges on the Wilbury Estate. At the time of the Second World War he served in the Cholderton Home Guard. This picture from the twenties, which shows John with his dog Jock, was kindly supplied by his daughter, Mrs Joan Newman of Allington.

THE OLD INN, ALLINGTON, at around the turn of the century. Harriet Burnett (the licensee) can be seen to the left with her son Frank and niece Bessy. We believe the man on the right to be Sammy Trass who lodged here at one time. The inn was destroyed by fire sometime before 1910 after which time the present Old Inn was built.

JAMES, ELIZABETH AND BARBARA STACEY, from a photograph taken just after the First World War. Before his days at Charles Farm (later known as Pages Farm), Allington, James was a blacksmith at Appleshaw in Hampshire, as was his father before him. He was also landlord of the Bell Inn which is known today as the Walnut Tree. One of four children (three girls and a boy), Barbara later became Mrs Penny.

THE DAUGHTERS DAY, but not all of them. Mabel had yet to be born. The eight young ladies pictured here in 1924 were the pride and joy of Ernest and Laura Day. The couple met at Tidworth when Ernest was a sergeant in the Royal Horse Artillery. Laura visited the garrison quite frequently when she collected and delivered laundry by horse and cart on behalf of her mother Sarah Amy Bevins, proprietress of Hillview Laundry. They fell in love and later married. Their first daughter, also named Laura, can be seen to the right, and then in descending order; Elsie, Dolly, Daisy, Dora (now Mrs Charlie Knight), Doris, Dulcie and Doreen.

A BOSCOMBE WORKINGMEN'S CLUB OUTING in the 1920s. To the extreme left of our photograph is Ben White, driver of this Albion coach and joint proprietor of Silver Star motor services. Some years ago he recognized many of the men who are pictured here: Allan Smith, Freddie Hatcher, John Smeeth, Ernie Mills, George Warriner, Archie Hunt, Paul Mouland, Jim Cannings, Ernest 'Shiner' Edmunds, Joe Day and two Blake brothers.

AN EDWARDIAN VIEW OF BOSCOMBE. The dwelling nearest to the camera we know today as Rosecott. Edwin Horner's horse-drawn cart from the Porton Supply Stores can be seen pulling into the lane which leads to The Old Rectory. Many years ago this quiet thoroughfare was on the main A338, Salisbury to Tidworth road.

BOSCOMBE POST OFFICE AND GROCERY STORE, before 1911. At the time of our photograph William J. Sheppard was the sub-postmaster and shopkeeper. His business was established towards the end of the last century and lasted for around twenty years. Mrs Susan Gavin took over from him and stayed until the later 1920s. By 1931, and well into the '50s the business was being managed by Miss Elsie May Miles. The services offered here were rather unbalanced. Money orders could be issued but they could not be cashed, and although wires were connected to the building there were no telegraph facilities (the nearest were at Porton). This is now a private dwelling named White Cottage.

BOSCOMBE AT THE TIME OF THE FIRST WORLD WAR. The post office shown on the opposite page can be seen again to the right of this picture. The motor car (AM 2623) was the conveyance of Canon George Biscoe Oldfield of Burroughs Hill, Laverstock. A very smart turnout, this 12/14 hp dark blue landaulette (lined out in gold) was manufactured by Scout Motors of Salisbury.

THE PLOUGH AT IDMISTON, in around 1908 when William Grant was the landlord. Little Boscombe can be seen in the distance. The following note appears on the back of our original photograph: 'Stopped here to rest our horse and give our driver a drink. Thought you would like this one for your album. We had our likeness taken at the Inn, will send one to you later.'

LOOKING DOWN ON IDMISTON. From a photographic postcard produced by May Brothers of Gomeldon Hill, Porton. Regular services are no longer held at All Saints' Church and only on special occasions is it reopened. When this picture was taken in 1906 the Revd George Mallows Youngman was the vicar. He lived at Porton.

IDMISTON TRINITY CLUB AT ALL SAINTS, in around 1888. It is never easy putting names to faces on a photograph of this age. We can, however, name Stephen Lawrence who can be seen to the right of the front row. Employed as a carter at Idmiston, Stephen died in 1904 at forty-four years of age.

MANOR HOUSE AND MANOR FARM, Idmiston in 1905. At the time of our photograph Richard Finch was residing at the Manor House and Reginald James Bacon was working Manor Farm. It would be almost impossible to record a similar view on a present-day camera because of all the new buildings and trees which occupy this area today.

HALE FARM HOUSE, Idmiston. Charles Marsh was the farm bailiff at around the time of the First World War when this photograph was taken. This farm, along with several others, was owned by Eustace Bertram Maton of Coombe Farm, Enford. We have not been able to positively identify the women in our picture. Do you know who they are?

GEORGE ALLEN AT HALE FARM, in the 1920s. George was born at East Burton near Wareham, Dorset on 15 March 1863 and died at Idmiston on 1 February 1936. He married Agnes 'Annie' Burgess (1868–1940), a native of Shanklin, Isle of Wight. George retired after working at Hale Farm for a number of years and he and Annie spent their last happy years together at Yew Tree Cottage, Idmiston.

Porton, Gomeldon, the Winterbournes and Hurdcott

THE SILVER STAR. We could not have found a more appropriate picture with which to start our tour of the villages in this section. The Silver Star motor service was founded in the early twenties by Eddie Shergold and Ben White. Eddie is shown here with the firm's first bus, a Ford Model T with an open-top, polished aluminium body by Pitt & Sons of Fordingbridge.

THE RAILWAY HOTEL AT PORTON in 1906 when Henry Foakes was manager. The horse-drawn tea van had travelled out from Lipton's of Silver Street, Salisbury. Most of the houses which can be seen in the background have survived.

THE RAILWAY HOTEL FIRE, 1921. At around 3 a.m. on Thursday 14 July, Captain Doggrell, his wife, three children and several guests were evacuated after a serious fire was discovered. The Salisbury Volunteer Fire Brigade dispatched their motor tender 'Fawcett' which arrived about an hour later.

THE SNUFF SHOP AND POST OFFICE at Porton in 1905. John Hawker, proprietor of the shop to the left of our picture, was licensed to sell snuff and tobacco (a modern building occupied by Porton Saddlery stands on the site today). The post and telegraph offices were managed by Arthur Ings.

THE KAIL FAMILY AND SHOP AT PORTON, after the First World War. Ernest Kail and his wife are pictured each side of the firm's Ford Model T van, and Hilda (later Mrs Charlie Tompkins) can be seen with Muriel (later Mrs Stone) in her arms. Wilfred is to the left and Ernie Bryant is to the right, with the horse and cart.

CHARLIE HILLIER AND MISS VOLLER at Porton station. Charlie was just a boy when he started working for the London and South Western Railway Company, he worked hard and made his way up to signalman. He lodged with Harry and Bessie Selway for many years.

THE CORONATION PARADE at Porton in June 1911. The Porton band, pictured here at Targett's Corner, lead the procession through the village, and from Buller Park to Birdlymes Home Park. In the afternoon several hundred people sat down to tea and the local children were each given a coronation mug.

THE BUICK. Henry George Targett of Birdlymes Farm, Porton, is pictured here with his post-war Buick tourer. Harry Parsons and Betsie can be seen to the right. The little white dog on the running-board answered to the name Jill.

THE TWELFTH ANNUAL BOURNE VALLEY FLOWER SHOW, held at Birdlymes Farm, Porton, in July 1905. The villagers pictured here are being entertained by Porton brass band. At the end of the day numerous prizes were presented by Messrs Richard Blake and Henry Targett.

THE ROAD GANG AT PORTON. We can only name two of these workmen: Tom Grinter is on the extreme left and Sid Moxham is fourth from the left. The van and drop-side trucks, which can be seen in the background, were pulled by a steam traction engine.

THE PORTON VAN. William Selway's carrier service was well established by 1907. A regular round trip was made from Porton to Salisbury for the Tuesday and Saturday markets. William stands to the right of our picture and his son Harry can be seen sitting on the van.

WEST GOMELDON AFTER THE STORM. On 25 April 1908 a most violent snowstorm lasting twelve hours swept across southern England. It was a breathtaking sight with drifts several feet deep in places. This was the heaviest fall since the great storm of January 1881.

MR SELWAY'S CAB AT GOMELDON, in around 1905. William Selway was a busy chap; besides running this cab he was the Porton carrier (see picture opposite) and coal merchant. The business, which passed to his son Harry during the 1920's, was still operating in the sixties.

GOMELDON COUNCIL SCHOOL, soon after the First World War. The school was built in 1913 to accommodate seventy-two children; the first headmistress was Miss B.S. Powell.

DANCING AROUND THE SCHOOL MAYPOLE, on Empire Day c. 1920. Miss Draper is pictured to the extreme right, next to Miss Strong, Miss Powell can be seen to the left. The two young girls at the front are Mercia Wright (later Mrs Light) and her friend Evelyn Bryant.

TRAVELLERS AT WEST GOMELDON in 1905. These colourful characters and their brightly painted caravans were regular visitors to the village. The thatched cottage to the right has long since gone but the house on the other side of the road has survived, although now much enlarged. This is presently known as The Gatehouse.

WINTERBOURNE CROSSROADS in 1904. The house to the left of our picture was demolished a long time ago. It is believed that a neighbourhood bobby lived here at one time. Could this be why the junction is now called Policeman's Corner? Ernie Dyke is the chap standing in the foreground.

WINTERBOURNE GUNNER POST OFFICE, before the First World War. Frances Pocock, sub-postmistress at the time of our photograph, can be seen in the doorway with her son Edwin (nicknamed Pat because he was born on St Patrick's Day). Pat's wife Hilda (née Pothecary) is still living in this house. The post office closed around thirty years ago.

THE NEW INN, WINTERBOURNE DAUNTSEY in 1905. Philip Tanswell was landlord in the last century, but at the time of our picture Fanny Agnes King was the registered keeper. When this road was widened a few years ago the inn was partly demolished and remodelled; it is now known as the Tything Man.

THE HARVEST TEA AT WINTERBOURNE EARLS in 1911. Around 200 parishioners are pictured here on the Vicarage lawn. After tea they were entertained by the Winterbourne String Band, and in the evening a thanksgiving service was held at St Michael's Church (beautifully decorated with flowers by Mrs Skyrme).

THE BAND, BICYCLES AND A BOBBY. On 4 June 1932 the annual Winterbourne Earls Fête was held to raise money to cover the cost of maintaining the children's playground. A sum was also set aside to benefit the elderly at Christmas. *En route* for Edwin Perrett's field, the Downton band are at the head of the procession.

WINTERBOURNE BAND, during the closing years of the last century. Sitting in front, to the left of the big drum, is bass drummer Frederick Bartlett (the only bandsman that we have been able to identify). For many years he was employed as a wheelwright at Winterbourne Gunner and his father, George, was a baker and grocer at Chitterne All Saints. The man wearing the bowler could be the band leader. He is wearing an eye patch and this could explain why he turned away from the camera.

RICHARD BLAKE AT THE ELMS, Winterbourne Earls, in 1897. Pictured left to right are: Philip Ings, Miss Baker (housekeeper), Mr Blake, John Ings, Mrs Blake (in the bathchair), Frances Ings and Bessie Ings.

THE CHURCH, THE SCHOOL AND A SHOP, taken in around 1916. The clock on St Michael's church was the gift of Richard Blake. At the time of our picture Albert William Hopkins was the resident master of the Elementary School (built around 120 years ago). We believe that the shop was managed by Mrs Louisa Stevens.

TWO EDWARDIAN VIEWS OF HURDCOTT. The thatched cottages, barns and the Wesleyan chapel have all disappeared and modern dwellings have been built here. The Black Horse Inn can be seen at the end of the lane in the lower picture (dated October 1904). The landlord at this time, John Williams, was also a blacksmith.

THRESHING AT GEORGE BRIGHT'S FARM in the twenties. This is where our journey ends. We hope you enjoyed it.

ACKNOWLEDGEMENTS

During a recent interview I was asked to express in a few words my opinion of the people of south Wiltshire with whom I had come into contact throughout my years of research. My response was instantaneous: 'They are friendly, generous, trusting, and genuinely interested.' I am pleased to say that out of the hundred or so individuals who were approached for pictures and/or information for *Around Amesbury In Old Photographs* only a few were unwilling to help.

In particular I am grateful to Mr Peter Goodhugh for his fine introduction, and to Mr E. Arthur Maidment for reading and correcting the proofs. Similarly, sincere thanks are offered to the following individuals and organizations who have helped in many different ways:

Bourne Valley Historical and Record Society.

Salisbury Journal and Times; David Eidlestein, Editor, and Daff Marriage, Chief Sub-editor.

Salisbury Museum; Peter Saunders, Curator, and Miss Clare Conybeare, Assistant Curator (Archaeology).

Salisbury Reference Library; Edward Boyle, Mrs Teresa Bowl and Miss Gillian Roberts.

Southern Evening Echo; Nigel Parkes, Chief Salisbury Reporter.

The Avon Advertiser; Ian Johnson, Editor.

Wiltshire Library and Museum Service; Local Studies Section.

Wiltshire Record Office.

Mrs Nelly Allen • Bill Allen • Alan Alexander • Charles Andrews
Sir Philip Antrobus Bt • Mrs Joan Arnold • Mrs Maurine Atkinson
Mrs Barbara Baillie • Andrew Baker • Ted Baker • Mrs Pat Beaver
Bob Bispham • Albert Brice • Mrs Caroline Bridger • Miss Mary Bridle
Mrs Rose Browning • Gerald Burden • Dennis Burgess • Dr John Chandler
Norman Chant • Mrs Stella Chant • Albert Chapel • Allen Chapman
Mrs Sylvia Chisman • Mrs Betty Coleman • Richard Cook • Alec Cooper
Richard C. Crook • Geoffrey Crowe • Harold Cruse • Mrs Mary Dixon
Mrs Freda Dudek • Mrs Thelma Duke • Gerald Futcher • Ian Gray
Mrs Phylis Greenhow • Mrs Janet Hall • Mrs May Hall • Mrs Dorothy Hardy
Sam Hart • Charles Hobson • Mrs M.E. Holmes • Mrs Doreen Hoxey
Ron Hurst • N.D.G. James • Mrs Patricia Jones • Mrs Roselle Jones
Mrs Joyce Kelly • Raymond Kite • Mrs Dora Knight • Mrs Mercia Light
Peter Maggs • Albert Mortimer • Mrs Joan Newman • Mrs Betty Osgood
Ernie Parsons • Bernard Pavey • Miss Joyce Pearce • Len Plank
Mrs Madge Powell • Mrs Angela Pryor • Mrs Edna Richardson
Mrs Olive Scarrott • Mrs V. Sheppard • David Smith • Mrs Kate Steele
Mrs Nelly Steele • Mrs Muriel Stone • Jim Swinton • Ken Thornton
Alan Toomer • Tony Tuff • Dave Underwood • Dave Ward • George Ward
Mrs Marilyn Watson • Tom Weeks • Jack Weston and Harry Withers.